ANIL KUMBLE COLOUR

MR VIVEK KUMAR PANDEY
SHAMBHUNATH

ISBN 979-888530554-9

Short biography of Anil Kumble and about life ,during writing this book no character & no religious are harmed written by Mr Vivek Kumar Pandey. winner youngest writer award 1st rank in india 2020.He is only one writer can publish 700+ own book that was greatest successfull in his life . this book fully colour edition books.

Contents

Foreword

Author biography in English :MY NAME IS VIVEK KUMAR PANDEY . I WAS BORN IN 30 SEP 2002,I AM FROM SURAT GUJARAT INDIA.MY DREAM WAS TO BE GOOD WRITERS ,MY FAMILY SUPPORTED ME TO SUCCESSFUL AND I CAN DO IT MY SELF.How do I write? That is a question, I believe, that cannot be honestly answered by me."CELEBRATING YOUNGEST WRITER AWARD WINNER IN GUJARAT 1ST RANK" MR PANDEY JI . I may think I did a good job writing something when in reality it could be horrible. The reader is the one who decides the quality of my writing. I do not find writing to be natural to me and therefore find it to be a real challenge. My trick as a challenged writer is to do the best I can and know that I am happy with the final outcome. It may take a while to do my best and there may be quite a few problems I run into along the way.

I am not a greedy person those who are thinking about me and my self I never tried it anyone people suffering from sadness ,I trying to get promoted people suffering from happiness and joy in your Life Time. Now in current situation in India and also world people are unemployed and have no many but our indian governor help to people to get free food from ration card , i also take part in leadership team ,i am Motivational speaker , Film script writer. There was my two dream firstly writer and secondly actor & also my own film is upcoming soon i done almost completely completed script for my film .I AM GOING TO SAY WORD OF HEART TOUCH OUT PLEASE READ IT" , firstly i thanks my father he supports me in this field they always getting inspired me by own his words and behavior ,they always said that he was a biggest person in the world in future and also they purchase fruit and chocolate for me in anytime & anyway , firstly my father buy him then call me Vivek you want a chocolate i will say yes papa but how many tell me ,papa: you tell me how much i buy him i told 1 or 2 chocolate but my father purchase whole the boxes of chocolate and they get suprised me. MY FATHER WAS BORN IN " 20 SEPTEMBER" 1971 IN INDIA.

1) MY FATHER FAVORITE CLOTHES IS KURTA PAIJMA AND ALSO STYLES SHOE

2) FAVORITE SINGER IS KISHORE DA

3) FAVORITE STATE GUJARAT AND KOLKATA , HIS VILLAGE IN BIHAR

4) FAVORITE COLOR BLACK AND WHITE

THEY ALSO LOVE cricket like IPL and one day t-20 .they also like watching a News daily and heard the song daily ,they also interested in tik tok video but in current time tik tok is banned in india but also few videos are in you tube. In lockdown time my family and me very enjoy day daily. my father play daily ludo with his sister and son, daughter.they always loved tea and coffee anytime call me "। वविक थोडा़ चाय बनाओना वविक तमुहारे हाथ का चाय अच्छा लगता है". I make it tea for my father but some reason after the April to june they are suffering from fever and cough , weakness on 6 June 2020 my father death. they not told me say bye bye his life. After death of 6 June on 10 june my mom and dad anniversary.but my father is Best in the world they can do anything for me please take care of father and respect it of your parents

CHAPTER ONE

Anil Kumble Colour

- Anil Kumble

1. During writing this book no character & no religious are harmed written by Mr Vivek Kumar Pandey.

Anil Kumble born 17 October 1970 is a former Indian cricket coach and commentator who played Test and One Day International cricket for his national team over an international career of 18 years. Widely regarded as one of the best leg spin bowlers in Test cricket history, he took 619 wickets in Test cricket and is the fourth highest wicket taker of all time as of 2021. In 1999 while playing against Pakistan, Kumble dismissed all ten batsmen in a Test match innings, joining England's Jim Laker as the second player to achieve the feat.Unlike his contemporaries, Kumble was not a big turner of the ball, but relied primarily on pace, bounce, and accuracy. He was nicknamed "Apple" and "Jumbo". Kumble was selected as the Cricketer of the Year in 1993 Indian Cricket, and one of the Wisden Cricketers of the Year three years later.

Born in Bangalore, Karnataka, Kumble developed an early interest in cricket as he grew up watching players like B. S. Chandrasekhar before becoming a full-fledged cricketer. He made his First-class debut at the age of 19 while representing Karnataka. Soon he was picked up for the Austral-Asia Cup in 1990 before making his Test debut against England later that year. Since then he has represented the Indian Test team on more than 132 Test matches and was responsible for many of India's victories. Kumble became a part of the regular ODI team during the early 1990s and held some of the best performances during this time; which included his six for 12 (six wickets for 12 runs) against the West Indies. The year 1996 proved to very successful for him as he was selected for the World Cup and emerged as the most successful bowler of the tournament; he played seven matches and captured 15 wickets at an average of 18.73.

Kumble was awarded the Padma Shri, India's fourth-highest civilian honour in 2005. After having played for 18 years, he announced his retirement from international cricket in November 2008. In October 2012, Kumble was appointed the chairman of the International Cricket Council (ICC)'s cricket committee.

Between 2012 and 2015, Kumble held positions as a chief mentor for the teams Royal Challengers Bangalore and Mumbai Indians in the Indian Premier League. He was also a former head coach of the Indian cricket team as well. In February 2015, he became the fourth Indian cricketer to be inducted into ICC Hall of Fame. Kumble is currently the Head Coach and the Director of Cricket Operations of Punjab Kings.

- Personal life

Kumble was born to family in Bangalore, Karnataka to Krishna Swamy and Saroja who both hail from Kumbla near Kasaragod, Kerala.Kumble has a brother named Diinesh Kumble. He is married to Chetana Kumble,and has three children – son Mayas Kumble and daughters Aaruni and Svasti Kumble. His mother tongue is Kannada.

Kumble's primary school was Holy Saint English School and he did his high schooling in National High School Basavanagudi. He began playing cricket on the streets of Bangalore and joined a club called "Young Cricketers" at the age of 13. He completed his pre-university education from National College Basavanagudi. Kumble graduated B.E from Rashtreeya Vidyalaya College of Engineering (RVCE) in Mechanical Engineering in 1991–92. He is nicknamed "Jumbo" not only because his deliveries, for a spinner, are "as fast as a jumbo jet", but also because his feet are quite big or "Jumbo" as observed by his teammates.

- Career

Early domestic career and international debut
Kumble made his first-class debut for Karnataka against Hyderabad on 30 November 1989, taking 4 wickets and bagging a pair. He was then selected for India Under-19s against Pakistan Under-19s, scoring 113 in the first test and 76 in the second. He made his ODI debut against Sri Lanka at Sharjah in the Austral-Asia Cup on 25 April 1990.He played one more game in the series against Pakistan and ended up picking two wickets. His Test debut came in the same year when India toured England for a three-test series.It was the second test of the series played at Manchester and he picked up 3 wickets conceding 105 runs in the first innings and went wicket-less in the second

innings of the match which resulted in a draw. He did not play any Tests until 1992. Kumble picked up 13/138 in Irani Trophy against Delhi for Rest of India which ensured the latter's victory.

This performance helped him earn a place in the Indian side that toured South Africa and Zimbabwe. It was during the 1992 Indian tour of South Africa that he established himself as a quality spinner, taking eight wickets in the second Test. All in all he took 18 wickets at an average of 25.94 and with an economy rate of 1.84 in the four-test series. Later that year, when England toured India, Kumble took 21 wickets in three Tests at an average of 19.8. He picked up seven wickets for 165 runs in the third Test of the series played at Bombay as India went on to win the match by an innings and 15 runs. He was adjudged man of the match for his performance.

Kumble took his first 50 Test wickets in 10 matches; the record remained the fastest by an Indian bowler till Ravichandran Ashwin surpassed him achieving the feat in nine matches. His 100 Test wickets in 21 Test matches, the second fastest by an Indian bowler after Erapalli Prasanna (who took 100 wickets in 20 matches). On 27 November 1993, he took six wickets for 12 runs in an ODI against the West Indies at Eden Gardens, Calcutta in the final of the Hero Cup, which was an Indian record for very long time. This record was broken by Stuart Binny on 17 June 2014 against Bangladesh.In January 1994, when Sri Lanka toured India, Kumble picked up his first 10 wicket haul in his 14th match which ensured India's victory by an innings and 119 runs. He picked up 11 wickets for 128 runs in the match.

In 1995 English cricket season Kumble played for Northamptonshire and was the leading wicket taker with 105 wickets at the average of 20.40. He was the only bowler to take more than 100 wickets during that season. His best performance came against Hampshire in a drawn match in County Championship, picking up 13 wickets for 192 runs.This performance in the English county cricket was noted by Wisden as they named him one of their five Cricketers of the Year in 1996.

- 1996 World Cup

Further information: 1996 Cricket World Cup
The year 1996 proved to be extremely successful for Kumble as he claimed 61 ODI wickets at an average of 20.24.All in all, he was the leading wicket-taker in the calendar year with 90 wickets at an average of 24.14 in Tests and ODIs combined. Kumble was selected in the Indian side for the 1996 World Cup. He was a part of all the seven matches that India played. Kumble was the leading wicket-taker in the tournament with 15 wickets at an average of 18.73. India played their first match against Kenya where Kumble took three for 28 runs, which helped to restrict Kenya for just 199/6 in their 50 overs. India won the match comfortably by seven wickets. In the subsequent matches he picked up three for 35 runs (against West Indies) and two wickets for 39 runs (against Sri Lanka) in group phase.

India played against Pakistan in the quarter-final phase. Kumble picked up 3 for 48 in the match which India eventually won. In the semi-final they subsequently lost to Sri Lanka in which Kumble's performance was 1 for 51.

- Setting records and rise through the ranks

Anil Kumble bowling in the Boxing Day Test Match at Melbourne

In October 1996, Anil Kumble along with Javagal Srinath helped India to win a scintillating ODI match against Australia in Bangalore in Titan Cup. The duo added 52 runs for 9th wicket partnership, after Sachin Tendulkar got out at 88 when India was 164/8, chasing a target of 216 runs. India eventually went on to win the Titan Cup. In February 1997 India visited the West Indies for a series of five tests and four ODIs.Kumble was part of the squad and he was the leading wicket-taker in the Test series. He picked up 19 wickets, averaging 30.31 with the ball. Kumble was the leading wicket-taker by a large margin when Australia visited India for Border-Gavaskar Trophy in 1998. He picked up 23 wickets in 3 test matches at the average of 18.26.

Kumble is one of three bowlers ever (the other two being Jim Laker of England in 1956 and Ajaz Patel of New Zealand in 2021) to have taken all ten wickets in a Test innings, taking 10 for 74. Kumble achieved this against Pakistan in the second Test played in Delhi in February 1999. Although by failing to dismiss Pakistan's Waqar Younis in either innings, he missed out on the achievement of dismissing all eleven batsmen in a Test match. It has been said that once he had got nine wickets his friend and teammate Javagal Srinath started bowling wide outside the off stump, so that Kumble could take the 10th.

The performance was rated by Wisden as the second best "Bowling performance of all time". The achievement was commemorated by naming a traffic circle in Bengaluru after him, and gifting him a car with the customized license plate: KA-10-N-10. In 1999 he was the third highest wicket taker with 88 wickets at the average of 30.03 behind Glenn

Mcgrath and Shane Warne.

When the Indian opener, Sadagoppan Ramesh tried to take a catch off Srinath, he was cautioned by Javagal Srinath not to try and take any catch so that Anil Kumble could take all 10 Wickets. This was revealed by Ramesh in an interview via 10 Sports; about the particular match "Anil Kumble's 10 wickets against Pakistan at Feroz Shah Kotla, New Delhi in 1999". When Kumble was looking to take his tenth wicket in the India-Pakistan test in 1999, Srinath, who was bowling from the other end, was trying to bowl way outside the off-stump to avoid taking the final wicket in order for Kumble to get to the record. Anil Kumble always gives full credit to him for his perfect 10 against Pakistan as Srinath bowled two wide balls in test match to avoid taking a wicket.

On 6 October 2004, Kumble became only the third spinner in the history of Test cricket after Shane Warne and Muttiah Muralitharan and the second Indian bowler after Kapil Dev to capture 400 Test wickets. Reaching the mark took him 30 fewer Test matches than it took Kapil Dev, and 7 fewer than Warne. In the India-West Indies series of 2006, Kumble took 6–78 in the second innings of the final Test in Sabina Park, Jamaica, and bowled India to a historic series win; it had been 35 years since a similar series victory. During the first innings of the match, Kumble scored 45 and became the second player in the history of the game after Shane Warne to score 2000 runs and take over 500 Test wickets. Kumble also holds the world record for trapping most batsmen leg before wicket. On 10 December 2004, Kumble became India's highest wicket-taker when he trapped Mohammad Rafique of Bangladesh to surpass Kapil Dev's haul of 434 wickets.

Kumble also played for ACC Asian XI against ICC World XI in World cricket tsunami appeal ODI match on 10 January 2005 held at the Melbourne cricket ground which was organised for the charity purpose for 2004 Indian Ocean earthquake and tsunami victims. In the match, he picked up 2/73 and scored 11 runs off 7 balls. For his performances in 2005, he was named as 12th man in the Test World Test XI by ICC.

Kumble claimed his 500th Test wicket in the Second Test of England's tour of India in March 2006, when he dismissed Steve Harmison lbw. He became the first Indian and fifth overall to reach the mark. After returning to India from the 2007 World Cup, he announced his retirement from ODIs, on 30 March.

On 10 August that year, Kumble scored his maiden Test century, making an unbeaten 110 against England at the Oval to help his team finish with 664. He took 118 Tests to reach his maiden Test hundred, which is a record for taking the most matches to score a century, beating Chaminda Vaas who had held this record previously with 96 Tests. It was also the only hundred by an Indian in the three-Test series.He is the only Test cricketer to have taken all ten wickets in an innings and score a Test hundred in his career. A day after scoring his ton, Kumble dismissed Vaughan for his 900th International wicket and 563rd Test wicket, drawing him level with McGrath. Later he trapped Monty Panesar for an lbw to finish the innings and overtake McGrath in the list of all-time wicket-takers, only Muttiah Muralitharan and Shane Warne have more wickets.

Kumble has bowled 40850 balls in his entire Test career, which is second highest after M Muralitharan's 44039 balls.

Kumble was appointed as the captain of the Indian Test cricket team on 8 November 2007. He succeeded his state teammate Rahul Dravid, who resigned as the captain in September 2007. He is the only leg spinner who have become the captain of the team. His first series as captain of Indian Test team was a three-match series against Pakistan played in India. which the team won by 1–0.

- Kumble bowling in a match against South Africa in 2008.

On 17 January 2008, in the third Test against Australia at WACA, Perth, Anil Kumble became the first Indian bowler and the third in the world to reach the milestone of 600 Test wickets. Kumble achieved the record just after the tea break when he had Andrew Symonds caught by Rahul Dravid at first slip. Kumble's 600 wickets came in 124 matches at an average of 28.68. Kumble has captured most wickets against Australia by an Indian bowler. Kumble is the third bowler after Muttiah Muralitharan and Shane Warne to take 600 Test wickets.

- Retirement from International cricket

Kumble injured the little finger of his left hand while attempting a catch off Matthew Hayden in Australia's first innings which rendered him unfit for the 4th and final test of the series against Australia in November 2008.Kumble was finding it difficult to find his striking form and went wicketless in four consecutive innings before the first innings of Australia in the third test of the series against Australia in which he managed three lower-order wickets. He declared the 2nd innings of India with only 6 overs of play left in the drawn match. His final figures were 4–0–14–0.

Anil Kumble announced his retirement from International test cricket, first-class cricket, and list A cricket appearances on 2 November 2008 in the 3rd Test match against Australia at Feroz Shah Kotla cricket stadium at New Delhi, India. He took the last wicket of his career of Mitchell Johnson.The final ball of his test career was a low full toss on which Matthew Hayden scored a four. After his retirement, Dhoni was made the captain of the team.

- IPL career

Kumble agreed to honour his contract with the Royal Challengers Bangalore (RCB) franchise of the Indian Premier League after retirement. He was given a three-year contract worth US$500,000 per year in the first round of bidding in 2008.

On 18 April 2009 he took a five-wicket haul conceding just 5 runs in 3.1 overs against the defending champions Rajasthan Royals, which helped RCB get a 75-run victory in the second match of the 2009 edition, played in South Africa. Even today, this remains the fourth-best bowling figures in IPL history. After the departure of Kevin Pietersen for England's cricket commitments, Kumble was named as the captain of the Royal Challengers. On 23 May 2009, his team defeated the Chennai Super Kings by six wickets and got a spot in the final against the Deccan Chargers. RCB lost the finals but Kumble won Man of the Match, and is the only person in IPL history to win Man of the Match in the finals despite being on the losing side. Though RCB could not win the tournament, Kumble ended as the most successful spin bowler and the 2nd highest wicket-taker of the tournament with 21 wickets at an economy rate of 5.86 runs per over behind R. P. Singh.

In 2010 Indian Premier League, Kumble led the team to the semi-finals. After being forced to play their semi-finals at the DY Patil Stadium following security concerns in Bangalore,the Royal Challengers lost their semi-final to the Mumbai Indianswith Kumble taking 1 wicket at an economy rate of 7.50 in the match. For his performances in 2010, he was named in the Cricinfo IPL XI.

Kumble announced his retirement from Indian Premier League on 4 January 2011. After his retirement from IPL as a player, RCB appointed him as the chief mentor for the team, where he led them to the 2011 Finals against the Chennai Super Kings. Kumble left that position in January 2013, moving to a similar role with the Mumbai Indians, which he quit in November 2015 after delivering them 2 titles in alternative years. He is currently the Director of Operations for the Punjab Kings.

- Style and technique

Test career batting performance of Anil Kumble.
Kumble is a right-arm leg spinner (legbreak googly) with an unorthodox style, most famous for his flipper. and a right-hand batsman He started his career as a fast bowler, which gave him a useful faster delivery. His unique bowling style can be attributed to matting pitches in Bangalore which assist top-spin and over-spin.

Kumble is one of the 4 bowlers, alongside Richard Hadlee, Shane Warne and Muttiah Muralitharan, and the only Indian bowler ever, to have taken 5 wickets in a Test innings more than 30 times. He also holds the world record for the largest number of caught-and-bowled dismissals in tests, 35 – which forms 5.65% of his total wickets. He is also one of 4 Indian bowlers to have conceded over 250 runs in a Test match, although he took 12 wickets in that match. He is known for bowling tirelessly, having bowled 72 overs in a Test innings once. He is also remembered for his tenacity in bowling even when injured, especially after an incident in a match against West Indies where, despite having his broken jaw being heavily taped, he came back and took the wicket of Brian Lara.

Kumble relies more on accuracy, variations and bounce rather than spinning the ball. Sambit Bal, the editor of Cricinfo, wrote, "That he [Kumble] has been an unusual spinner has been said many times before. It has also been said, a trifle unfairly, that he is a unidimensional bowler. Palpably, he has lacked the turn of Warne and Murali, but his variety has been subtler, far more apparent to batsmen than to viewers. He has shown that not only turn and flight that can deceive the batsman but also the changes of length and pace. He has been a cultured practitioner of his unique craft and a master of nuances."As a captain and coach, he is a firm supporter of DRS.

• Involvement in cricket associations

Kumble has been appointed to the athlete's commission of the World Anti-Doping Agency (WADA), with his term starting on 1 January 2009.

On 21 November 2010, Kumble was elected as The President of the Karnataka State Cricket Association, with statemates and former India teammate Venkatesh Prasad elected as vice-president whereas his former teammate, Javagal Srinath got elected as Secretary.

On 12 Oct 2012, Kumble was appointed as the new Chairman of ICC Cricket Committee.Kumble has been retained as the chairman of the ICC Cricket Committee for another three years on 2 March 2019.

- Coaching career

On 24 June 2016 he was appointed as the head coach of the Indian Cricket Team by BCCI for a period of one year but resigned due to untenable differences with the captain, Virat Kohli, as stated by him. Anil Kumble's term of one year ended after the 2017 ICC Champions Trophy. The chief of COA, Vinod Rai, announced on 12 June 2017 that Anil Kumble will continue as the coach of the India Cricket Team for the upcoming West Indies tour of India. After a recent defeat in ICC Champions Trophy Final 2017 against Pakistan, he stepped down as the head coach of the Indian Cricket Team on 20 June 2017 after a duration of less than 1 year.

Kumble's first series as a coach was against the West Indies in July where India played four Test matches, winning 2–0. Later India beat New Zealand 3–0 in the Test series, his second consecutive Test series win as a coach. India also defeated England 4–0 in the five-Test series in November–December and stretched their winning streak to three test series victory under Kumble as a coach. India's fourth Test series win came against Bangladesh. India went on to dominate on their home soil which marked as India's 19-match unbeaten record in Tests. During the four-match Test series against Australia in March; India lost the first match but made a sensational comeback, beating the Australians in two of the last three tests, drawing one match and winning the series 2–1. India also registered two one-day series wins under Kumble's tenure, as India defeated New Zealand in a five one-day match series 3–2, followed by a 2–1 win over England in a three-match series.

Twitter statement by Kumble on 20 June 2017 – "I am honoured by the confidence reposed in me by the CAC, in asking me to continue as Head Coach. The credit for the achievements of the last one year goes to the Captain, the entire team, coaching and support staff. Post this intimation, I was informed for the first time yesterday by the BCCI that the Captain had reservations with my 'style' and about my continuing as the Head Coach. I was surprised since I have always respected the role boundaries between Captain and Coach. Though the BCCI attempted to resolve the misunderstandings between the Captain and me, it was apparent that the partnership was untenable, and I therefore believe it is best for me to move on. Professionalism, discipline, commitment, honesty, complementary skills and diverse views are the key traits I bring to the table. These need to be valued for the partnership to be effective. I see the Coach's role akin to 'holding a mirror' to drive self-improvement in the team's interest. In light of these 'reservations' I believe it is best I hand over this responsibility to whomever the CAC and BCCI deem fit. Let me reiterate that it has been an absolute privilege to have served as Head Coach for the last one year. I thank the CAC, BCCI, CoA, and all concerned. I also wish to thank the innumerable followers and fans of Indian cricket for their continued support. I will remain a well-wisher of the great cricketing tradition of my country forever."

In October 2019, he was appointed as the Head Coach and the Director of Cricket Operations for Kings XI Punjab.

- Awards and honours

1. Arjuna award, a sports award from the Government of India, in 1995

2. One of the Wisden Cricketers of the Year, in 1996.

3. Among the 16 cricketers shortlisted for the Wisden Indian Cricketer of the 20th Century, in 2002 (Kapil Dev won)

4. Padma Shri, a civilian award from the Government of India, in 2005.

5. A prominent intersection in M. G. Road, Bengaluru has been named after Anil Kumble.

6. 'Best breakthrough performance IPL 2009' for his five-for-five against Rajasthan Royals in IPL 2009.

7. ICC Cricket Hall of Fame, a sports award from the ICC, in 2015.

CHAPTER TWO

Let's Know About Cricket

- Cricket

Cricket is a bat-and-ball game played between two teams of eleven players on a field at the centre of which is a 22-yard (20-metre) pitch with a wicket at each end, each comprising two bails balanced on three stumps. The game proceeds when a player on the fielding team, called the bowler, "bowls" (propels) the ball from one end of the pitch towards the wicket at the other end. The batting side's players score runs by striking the bowled ball with a bat and running between the wickets, while the bowling side tries to prevent this by keeping the ball within the field and getting it to either wicket, and dismiss each batter (so they are "out"). Means of dismissal include being bowled, when the ball hits the stumps and dislodges the bails, and by the fielding side either catching a hit ball before it touches the ground, or hitting a wicket with the ball before a batter can cross the crease line in front of the wicket to complete a run. When ten batters have been dismissed, the innings ends and the teams swap roles. The game is adjudicated by two umpires, aided by a third umpire and match referee in international matches.

Forms of cricket range from Twenty20, with each team batting for a single innings of 20 overs and the game generally lasting three hours, to Test matches played over five days. Traditionally cricketers play in all-white kit, but in limited overs cricket they wear club or team colours. In addition to the basic kit, some players wear protective gear to prevent injury caused by the ball, which is a hard, solid spheroid made of compressed leather with a slightly raised sewn seam enclosing a cork core layered with tightly wound string.

The earliest reference to cricket is in South East England in the mid-16th century. It spread globally with the expansion of the British Empire, with the first international matches in the second half of the 19th century. The game's governing body is the International Cricket Council (ICC), which has over 100 members, twelve of which are full members who play Test matches. The game's rules, the Laws of Cricket, are maintained by Marylebone Cricket Club (MCC) in London. The sport is followed primarily in South Asia, Australasia, the United Kingdom, southern Africa and the West Indies.Women's cricket, which is organised and played separately, has also achieved international standard. The most successful side playing international cricket is Australia, which has won seven One Day International trophies, including five World Cups, more than any other country and has been the top-rated Test side more than any other country.

- History of cricket to 1725

A medieval "club ball" game involving an underhand bowl towards a batter. Ball catchers are shown positioning themselves to catch a ball. Detail from the Canticles of Holy Mary, 13th century.

Cricket is one of many games in the "club ball" sphere that basically involve hitting a ball with a hand-held implement; others include baseball (which shares many similarities with cricket, both belonging in the more specific bat-and-ball games category), golf, hockey, tennis, squash, badminton and table tennis. In cricket's case, a key difference is the existence of a solid target structure, the wicket (originally, it is thought, a "wicket gate" through which sheep were herded), that the batter must defend. The cricket historian Harry Altham identified three "groups" of "club ball" games: the "hockey group", in which the ball is driven to and fro between two targets (the goals); the "golf group", in which the ball is driven towards an undefended target (the hole); and the "cricket group", in which "the ball is aimed at a mark (the wicket) and driven away from it".

It is generally believed that cricket originated as a children's game in the south-eastern counties of England, sometime during the medieval period.Although there are claims for prior dates, the earliest definite reference to cricket being played comes from evidence given at a court case in Guildford in January 1597 (Old Style), equating to January 1598 in the modern calendar. The case concerned ownership of a certain plot of land and the court heard the testimony of a 59-year-old coroner, John Derrick, who gave witness that.

Being a scholler in the ffree schoole of Guldeford hee and diverse of his fellows did runne and play there at creckett and other plaies.

Given Derrick's age, it was about half a century earlier when he was at school and so it is certain that cricket was being played c. 1550 by boys in Surrey. The view that it was originally a children's game is reinforced by Randle Cotgrave's 1611 English-French dictionary in which he defined the noun "crosse" as "the crooked staff wherewith boys play at cricket" and the verb form "crosser" as "to play at cricket".

One possible source for the sport's name is the Old English word "cryce" (or "cricc") meaning a crutch or staff. In Samuel Johnson's Dictionary, he derived cricket from "cryce, Saxon, a stick". In Old French, the word "criquet" seems to have meant a kind of club or stick. Given the strong medieval trade connections between south-east England and the County of Flanders when the latter belonged to the Duchy of Burgundy, the name may have been derived from the Middle Dutch (in use in Flanders at the time) "krick"(-e), meaning a stick (crook). Another possible source is the Middle Dutch word "krickstoel", meaning a long low stool used for kneeling in church and which resembled the long low wicket with two stumps used in early cricket. According to Heiner Gillmeister, a European language expert of Bonn University, "cricket" derives from the Middle Dutch phrase for hockey, met de (krik ket)sen (i.e., "with the stick chase"). Gillmeister has suggested that not only the name but also the sport itself may be of Flemish origin.

- Growth of amateur and professional cricket in England

Evolution of the cricket bat. The original "hockey stick" (left) evolved into the straight bat from c. 1760 when pitched delivery bowling began.

Although the main object of the game has always been to score the most runs, the early form of cricket differed from the modern game in certain key technical aspects; the North American variant of cricket known as wicket retained many of these aspects. The ball was bowled underarm by the bowler and along the ground towards a batter armed with a bat that in shape resembled a hockey stick; the batter defended a low, two-stump wicket; and runs were called notches because the scorers recorded them by notching tally sticks.

In 1611, the year Cotgrave's dictionary was published, ecclesiastical court records at Sidlesham in Sussex state that two parishioners, Bartholomew Wyatt and Richard Latter, failed to attend church on Easter Sunday because they were playing cricket. They were fined 12d each and ordered to do penance.This is the earliest mention of adult participation in cricket and it was around the same time that the earliest known organised inter-parish or village match was played – at Chevening, Kent. In 1624, a player called Jasper Vinall died after he was accidentally struck on the head during a match between two parish teams in Sussex.

Cricket remained a low-key local pursuit for much of the 17th century. It is known, through numerous references found in the records of ecclesiastical court cases, to have been proscribed at times by the Puritans before and during the Commonwealth. The problem was nearly always the issue of Sunday play as the Puritans considered cricket to be "profane" if played on the Sabbath, especially if large crowds or gambling were involved.

According to the social historian Derek Birley, there was a "great upsurge of sport after the Restoration" in 1660. Gambling on sport became a problem significant enough for Parliament to pass the 1664 Gambling Act, limiting stakes to £100 which was, in any case, a colossal sum exceeding the annual income of 99% of the population. Along with prizefighting, horse racing and blood sports, cricket was perceived to be a gambling sport.Rich patrons made matches for high stakes, forming teams in which they engaged the first professional players.By the end of the century, cricket had developed into a major sport that was spreading throughout England and was already being taken abroad by English mariners and colonisers – the earliest reference to cricket overseas is dated 1676. A 1697 newspaper report survives of "a great cricket match" played in Sussex "for fifty guineas apiece" – this is the earliest known contest that is generally considered a First Class match.

- The patrons, and other players from the social class known as the "gentry", began to classify themselves as "amateurs"[fn 1] to establish a clear distinction from the professionals, who were invariably members of the working class, even to the point of having separate changing and dining facilities. The gentry, including such high-ranking nobles as the Dukes of Richmond, exerted their honour code of noblesse oblige to claim rights of leadership in any sporting contests they took part in, especially as it was necessary for them to play alongside their "social inferiors" if they were to win their bets. In time, a perception took hold that the typical amateur who played in first-class cricket, until 1962 when amateurism was abolished, was someone with a public school education who had then gone to one of Cambridge or Oxford University – society insisted that such people were "officers and gentlemen" whose destiny was to provide leadership. In a purely financial sense, the cricketing amateur would theoretically claim expenses for playing while his professional counterpart played under contract and was paid a wage or match fee; in practice, many amateurs claimed more than actual expenditure and the derisive term "shamateur" was coined to describe the practice.

- The Young Cricketer, 1768

The game underwent major development in the 18th century to become England's national sport.Its success was underwritten by the twin necessities of patronage and betting. Cricket was prominent in London as early as 1707 and, in the middle years of the century, large crowds flocked to matches on the Artillery Ground in Finsbury. The single wicket form of the sport attracted huge crowds and wagers to match, its popularity peaking in the 1748 season. Bowling underwent an evolution around 1760 when bowlers began to pitch the ball instead of rolling or skimming it towards the batter. This caused a revolution in bat design because, to deal with the bouncing ball, it was necessary to introduce the modern straight bat in place of the old "hockey stick" shape.

The Hambledon Club was founded in the 1760s and, for the next twenty years until the formation of Marylebone Cricket Club (MCC) and the opening of Lord's Old Ground in 1787, Hambledon was both the game's greatest club and its focal point. MCC quickly became the sport's premier club and the custodian of the Laws of Cricket. New Laws introduced in the latter part of the 18th century included the three stump wicket and leg before wicket (lbw).

The 19th century saw underarm bowling superseded by first roundarm and then overarm bowling. Both developments were controversial.Organisation of the game at county level led to the creation of the county clubs, starting with Sussex in 1839. In December 1889, the eight leading county clubs formed the official County Championship, which began in 1890.

The most famous player of the 19th century was W. G. Grace, who started his long and influential career in 1865. It was especially during the career of Grace that the distinction between amateurs and professionals became blurred by the existence of players like him who were nominally amateur but, in terms of their financial gain, de facto professional. Grace himself was said to have been paid more money for playing cricket than any professional.

The last two decades before the First World War have been called the "Golden Age of cricket". It is a nostalgic name prompted by the collective sense of loss resulting from the war, but the period did produce some great players and memorable matches, especially as organised competition at county and Test level developed.

- Cricket becomes an international sport

In 1844, the first-ever international match took place between the United States and Canada. In 1859, a team of English players went to North America on the first overseas tour. Meanwhile, the British Empire had been instrumental in spreading the game overseas and by the middle of the 19th century it had become well established in Australia, the Caribbean, India, Pakistan, New Zealand, North America and South Africa.

In 1862, an English team made the first tour of Australia. The first Australian team to travel overseas consisted of Aboriginal stockmen who toured England in 1868. The first One Day International match was played on 5 January 1971 between Australia and England at the Melbourne Cricket Ground.

In 1876–77, an England team took part in what was retrospectively recognised as the first-ever Test match at the Melbourne Cricket Ground against Australia. The rivalry between England and Australia gave birth to The Ashes in 1882, and this has remained Test cricket's most famous contest. Test cricket began to expand in 1888–89 when South Africa played England.

- World cricket in the 20th century

The inter-war years were dominated by Australia's Don Bradman, statistically the greatest Test batter of all time. Test cricket continued to expand during the 20th century with the addition of the West Indies (1928), New Zealand (1930) and India (1932) before the Second World War and then Pakistan (1952), Sri Lanka (1982), Zimbabwe (1992), Bangladesh (2000), Ireland and Afghanistan (both 2018) in the post-war period. South Africa was banned from international cricket from 1970 to 1992 as part of the apartheid boycott.

- The rise of limited overs cricket

Cricket entered a new era in 1963 when English counties introduced the limited overs variant. As it was sure to produce a result, limited overs cricket was lucrative and the number of matches increased. The first Limited

Overs International was played in 1971 and the governing International Cricket Council (ICC), seeing its potential, staged the first limited overs Cricket World Cup in 1975. In the 21st century, a new limited overs form, Twenty20, made an immediate impact. On 22 June 2017, Afghanistan and Ireland became the 11th and 12th ICC full members, enabling them to play Test cricket.

- A typical cricket field.

In cricket, the rules of the game are specified in a code called The Laws of Cricket (hereinafter called "the Laws") which has a global remit. There are 42 Laws (always written with a capital "L"). The earliest known version of the code was drafted in 1744 and, since 1788, it has been owned and maintained by its custodian, the Marylebone Cricket Club (MCC) in London.

- Playing area

Cricket is a bat-and-ball game played on a cricket field between two teams of eleven players each. The field is usually circular or oval in shape and the edge of the playing area is marked by a boundary, which may be a fence, part of the stands, a rope, a painted line or a combination of these; the boundary must if possible be marked along its entire length.

In the approximate centre of the field is a rectangular pitch (see image, below) on which a wooden target called a wicket is sited at each end; the wickets are placed 22 yards (20 m) apart. The pitch is a flat surface 10 feet (3.0 m) wide, with very short grass that tends to be worn away as the game progresses (cricket can also be played on artificial surfaces, notably matting). Each wicket is made of three wooden stumps topped by two bails.

- Cricket pitch and creases

As illustrated above, the pitch is marked at each end with four white painted lines: a bowling crease, a popping crease and two return creases. The three stumps are aligned centrally on the bowling crease, which is eight feet eight inches long. The popping crease is drawn four feet in front of the bowling crease and parallel to it; although it is drawn as a twelve-foot line (six feet either side of the wicket), it is, in fact, unlimited in length. The return creases are drawn at right angles to the popping crease so that they intersect the ends of the bowling crease; each return crease is drawn as an eight-foot line, so that it extends four feet behind the bowling crease, but is also, in fact, unlimited in length.

Before a match begins, the team captains (who are also players) toss a coin to decide which team will bat first and so take the first innings. Innings is the term used for each phase of play in the match.In each innings, one team bats, attempting to score runs, while the other team bowls and fields the ball, attempting to restrict the scoring and dismiss the batters. When the first innings ends, the teams change roles; there can be two to four innings depending upon the type of match. A match with four scheduled innings is played over three to five days; a match with two scheduled innings is usually completed in a single day. During an innings, all eleven members of the fielding team take the field, but usually only two members of the batting team are on the field at any given time. The exception to this is if a batter has any type of illness or injury restricting his or her ability to run, in this case the batter is allowed a runner who can run between the wickets when the batter hits a scoring run or runs,though this does not apply in international cricket. The order of batters is usually announced just before the match, but it can be varied.

The main objective of each team is to score more runs than their opponents but, in some forms of cricket, it is also necessary to dismiss all of the opposition batters in their final innings in order to win the match, which would otherwise be drawn. If the team batting last is all out having scored fewer runs than their opponents, they are said to have "lost by n runs" (where n is the difference between the aggregate number of runs scored by the teams). If the team that bats last scores enough runs to win, it is said to have "won by n wickets", where n is the number of wickets left to fall. For example, a team that passes its opponents' total having lost six wickets (i.e., six of their batters have been dismissed) have won the match "by four wickets".

In a two-innings-a-side match, one team's combined first and second innings total may be less than the other side's first innings total. The team with the greater score is then said to have "won by an innings and n runs", and does not need to bat again: n is the difference between the two teams' aggregate scores. If the team batting last is all out, and both sides have scored the same number of runs, then the match is a tie; this result is quite rare in matches of two innings a side with only 62 happening in first-class matches from the earliest known instance in 1741 until January 2017. In the traditional form of the game, if the time allotted for the match expires before either side can win, then the game is declared a draw.

If the match has only a single innings per side, then a maximum number of overs applies to each innings. Such a match is called a "limited overs" or "one-day" match, and the side scoring more runs wins regardless of the number of wickets lost, so that a draw cannot occur. In some cases, ties are broken by having each team bat for a one-over innings known as a Super Over; subsequent Super Overs may be played if the first Super Over ends in a tie. If this kind of match is temporarily interrupted by bad weather, then a complex mathematical formula, known as the Duckworth–Lewis–Stern method after its developers, is often used to recalculate a new target score. A one-day match can also be declared a "no-result" if fewer than a previously agreed number of overs have been bowled by either team, in circumstances that make normal resumption of play impossible; for example, wet weather.

In all forms of cricket, the umpires can abandon the match if bad light or rain makes it impossible to continue. There have been instances of entire matches, even Test matches scheduled to be played over five days, being lost to bad weather without a ball being bowled: for example, the third Test of the 1970/71 series in Australia.

- Innings

The innings (ending with 's' in both singular and plural form) is the term used for each phase of play during a match. Depending on the type of match being played, each team has either one or two innings. Sometimes all eleven members of the batting side take a turn to bat but, for various reasons, an innings can end before they have all done so. The innings terminates if the batting team is "all out", a term defined by the Laws: "at the fall of a wicket or the retirement of a batter, further balls remain to be bowled but no further batter is available to come in". In this situation, one of the batters has not been dismissed and is termed not out; this is because he has no partners left and there must always be two active batters while the innings is in progress.

- An innings may end early while there are still two not out batters

the batting team's captain may declare the innings closed even though some of his players have not had a turn to bat: this is a tactical decision by the captain, usually because he believes his team have scored sufficient runs and need time to dismiss the opposition in their innings

the set number of overs (i.e., in a limited overs match) have been bowled

the match has ended prematurely due to bad weather or running out of time

in the final innings of the match, the batting side has reached its target and won the game.

- Overs

The Laws state that, throughout an innings, "the ball shall be bowled from each end alternately in overs of 6 balls". The name "over" came about because the umpire calls "Over!" when six balls have been bowled. At this point, another bowler is deployed at the other end, and the fielding side changes ends while the batters do not. A bowler cannot bowl two successive overs, although a bowler can (and usually does) bowl alternate overs, from the same end, for several overs which are termed a "spell". The batters do not change ends at the end of the over, and so the one who was non-striker is now the striker and vice versa. The umpires also change positions so that the one who was at "square leg" now stands behind the wicket at the non-striker's end and vice versa.

- Clothing and equipment

English cricketer W. G. Grace "taking guard" in 1883. His pads and bat are very similar to those used today. The gloves have evolved somewhat. Many modern players use more defensive equipment than were available to Grace, most notably helmets and arm guards.

The wicket-keeper (a specialised fielder behind the batter) and the batters wear protective gear because of the hardness of the ball, which can be delivered at speeds of more than 145 kilometres per hour (90 mph) and presents a major health and safety concern. Protective clothing includes pads (designed to protect the knees and shins), batting gloves or wicket-keeper's gloves for the hands, a safety helmet for the head and a box for male players inside the trousers (to protect the crotch area). Some batters wear additional padding inside their shirts and trousers such as thigh pads, arm pads, rib protectors and shoulder pads. The only fielders allowed to wear protective gear are those in positions very close to the batter (i.e., if they are alongside or in front of him), but they cannot wear gloves or external leg guards.

Subject to certain variations, on-field clothing generally includes a collared shirt with short or long sleeves; long trousers; woolen pullover (if needed); cricket cap (for fielding) or a safety helmet; and spiked shoes or boots to increase traction. The kit is traditionally all white and this remains the case in Test and first-class cricket but, in limited overs cricket, team colours are worn instead.

- Bat and ball

Two types of cricket ball, both of the same size:

i) A used white ball. White balls are mainly used in limited overs cricket, especially in matches played at night, under floodlights (left).

ii) A used red ball. Red balls are used in Test cricket, first-class cricket and some other forms of cricket (right).

The essence of the sport is that a bowler delivers (i.e., bowls) the ball from his or her end of the pitch towards the batter who, armed with a bat, is "on strike" at the other end (see next sub-section: Basic gameplay).

The bat is made of wood, usually Salix alba (white willow), and has the shape of a blade topped by a cylindrical handle. The blade must not be more than 4.25 inches (10.8 cm) wide and the total length of the bat not more than 38 inches (97 cm). There is no standard for the weight, which is usually between 2 lb 7 oz and 3 lb (1.1 and 1.4 kg).

The ball is a hard leather-seamed spheroid, with a circumference of 9 inches (23 cm). The ball has a "seam": six rows of stitches attaching the leather shell of the ball to the string and cork interior. The seam on a new ball is prominent and helps the bowler propel it in a less predictable manner. During matches, the quality of the ball deteriorates to a point where it is no longer usable; during the course of this deterioration, its behaviour in flight will change and can influence the outcome of the match. Players will, therefore, attempt to modify the ball's behaviour by modifying its physical properties. Polishing the ball and wetting it with sweat or saliva is legal, even when the polishing is deliberately done on one side only to increase the ball's swing through the air, but the acts of rubbing other substances into the ball, scratching the surface or picking at the seam are illegal ball tampering.

• Player roles

Basic gameplay: bowler to batter
During normal play, thirteen players and two umpires are on the field. Two of the players are batters and the rest are all eleven members of the fielding team. The other nine players in the batting team are off the field in the pavilion. The image with overlay below shows what is happening when a ball is being bowled and which of the personnel are on or close to the pitch.

• Return crease

In the photo, the two batters (3 & 8; wearing yellow) have taken position at each end of the pitch (6). Three members of the fielding team (4, 10 & 11; wearing dark blue) are in shot. One of the two umpires (1; wearing white hat) is stationed behind the wicket (2) at the bowler's (4) end of the pitch. The bowler (4) is bowling the ball (5) from his end of the pitch to the batter at the other end who is called the "striker". The other batter (3) at the bowling end is called the "non-striker". The wicket-keeper (10), who is a specialist, is positioned behind the striker's wicket (9) and behind him stands one of the fielders in a position called "first slip" (11). While the bowler and the first slip are wearing conventional kit only, the two batters and the wicket-keeper are wearing protective gear including safety helmets, padded gloves and leg guards (pads).
While the umpire (1) in shot stands at the bowler's end of the pitch, his colleague stands in the outfield, usually in

or near the fielding position called "square leg", so that he is in line with the popping crease (7) at the striker's end of the pitch. The bowling crease (not numbered) is the one on which the wicket is located between the return creases (12). The bowler (4) intends to hit the wicket (9) with the ball (5) or, at least, to prevent the striker (8) from scoring runs. The striker (8) intends, by using his bat, to defend his wicket and, if possible, to hit the ball away from the pitch in order to score runs.

Some players are skilled in both batting and bowling, or as either or these as well as wicket-keeping, so are termed all-rounders. Bowlers are classified according to their style, generally as fast bowlers, seam bowlers or spinners. Batters are classified according to whether they are right-handed or left-handed.

- Fielding

Of the eleven fielders, three are in shot in the image above. The other eight are elsewhere on the field, their positions determined on a tactical basis by the captain or the bowler. Fielders often change position between deliveries, again as directed by the captain or bowler.

If a fielder is injured or becomes ill during a match, a substitute is allowed to field instead of him, but the substitute cannot bowl or act as a captain, except in the case of concussion substitutes in international cricket. The substitute leaves the field when the injured player is fit to return. The Laws of Cricket were updated in 2017 to allow substitutes to act as wicket-keepers.

- Bowling and dismissal

Glenn McGrath of Australia holds the world record for most wickets in the Cricket World Cup.

Most bowlers are considered specialists in that they are selected for the team because of their skill as a bowler, although some are all-rounders and even specialist batters bowl occasionally. The specialists bowl several times during an innings but may not bowl two overs consecutively. If the captain wants a bowler to "change ends", another bowler must temporarily fill in so that the change is not immediate.

A bowler reaches his delivery stride by means of a "run-up" and an over is deemed to have begun when the bowler starts his run-up for the first delivery of that over, the ball then being "in play".

Fast bowlers, needing momentum, take a lengthy run up while bowlers with a slow delivery take no more than a couple of steps before bowling. The fastest bowlers can deliver the ball at a speed of over 145 kilometres per hour (90 mph) and they sometimes rely on sheer speed to try to defeat the batter, who is forced to react very quickly.

Other fast bowlers rely on a mixture of speed and guile by making the ball seam or swing (i.e. curve) in flight. This type of delivery can deceive a batter into miscuing his shot, for example, so that the ball just touches the edge of the bat and can then be "caught behind" by the wicket-keeper or a slip fielder. At the other end of the bowling scale is the spin bowler who bowls at a relatively slow pace and relies entirely on guile to deceive the batter. A spinner will often "buy his wicket" by "tossing one up" (in a slower, steeper parabolic path) to lure the batter into making a poor shot. The batter has to be very wary of such deliveries as they are often "flighted" or spun so that the ball will not behave quite as he expects and he could be "trapped" into getting himself out. In between the pacemen and the spinners are the medium paced seamers who rely on persistent accuracy to try to contain the rate of scoring and wear down the batter's concentration.

There are nine ways in which a batter can be dismissed: five relatively common and four extremely rare. The common forms of dismissal are bowled, caught, leg before wicket (lbw), run out and stumped. Rare methods are hit wicket,hit the ball twice, obstructing the field and timed out. The Laws state that the fielding team, usually the bowler in practice, must appeal for a dismissal before the umpire can give his decision. If the batter is out, the umpire raises a forefinger and says "Out!"; otherwise, he will shake his head and say "Not out".There is, effectively, a tenth method of dismissal, retired out, which is not an on-field dismissal as such but rather a retrospective one for which no fielder is credited.

- Batting, runs and extras

The directions in which a right-handed batter, facing down the page, intends to send the ball when playing various cricketing shots. The diagram for a left-handed batter is a mirror image of this one.

Batters take turns to bat via a batting order which is decided beforehand by the team captain and presented to the umpires, though the order remains flexible when the captain officially nominates the team. Substitute batters are generally not allowed, except in the case of concussion substitutes in international cricket.

In order to begin batting the batter first adopts a batting stance. Standardly, this involves adopting a slight crouch with the feet pointing across the front of the wicket, looking in the direction of the bowler, and holding the bat so it passes over the feet and so its tip can rest on the ground near to the toes of the back foot.

A skilled batter can use a wide array of "shots" or "strokes" in both defensive and attacking mode. The idea is to hit the ball to the best effect with the flat surface of the bat's blade. If the ball touches the side of the bat it is called an "edge". The batter does not have to play a shot and can allow the ball to go through to the wicketkeeper. Equally, he does not have to attempt a run when he hits the ball with his bat. Batters do not always seek to hit the ball as hard as possible, and a good player can score runs just by making a deft stroke with a turn of the wrists or by simply "blocking" the ball but directing it away from fielders so that he has time to take a run. A wide variety of shots are played, the batter's repertoire including strokes named according to the style of swing and the direction aimed: e.g., "cut", "drive", "hook", "pull".

The batter on strike (i.e. the "striker") must prevent the ball hitting the wicket, and try to score runs by hitting the ball with his bat so that he and his partner have time to run from one end of the pitch to the other before the fielding side can return the ball. To register a run, both runners must touch the ground behind the popping crease with either their bats or their bodies (the batters carry their bats as they run). Each completed run increments the score of both the team and the striker.

- Sachin Tendulkar is the only player to have scored one hundred international centuries

The decision to attempt a run is ideally made by the batter who has the better view of the ball's progress, and this is communicated by calling: usually "yes", "no" or "wait". More than one run can be scored from a single hit: hits worth one to three runs are common, but the size of the field is such that it is usually difficult to run four or more. To compensate for this, hits that reach the boundary of the field are automatically awarded four runs if the ball touches the ground en route to the boundary or six runs if the ball clears the boundary without touching the ground within the boundary. In these cases the batters do not need to run. Hits for five are unusual and generally rely on the help of "overthrows" by a fielder returning the ball. If an odd number of runs is scored by the striker, the two batters have changed ends, and the one who was non-striker is now the striker. Only the striker can score individual runs, but all runs are added to the team's total.

Additional runs can be gained by the batting team as extras (called "sundries" in Australia) due to errors made by the fielding side. This is achieved in four ways: no-ball, a penalty of one extra conceded by the bowler if he breaks the rules; wide, a penalty of one extra conceded by the bowler if he bowls so that the ball is out of the batter's reach bye, an extra awarded if the batter misses the ball and it goes past the wicket-keeper and gives the batters time to run in the conventional way leg bye, as for a bye except that the ball has hit the batter's body, though not his bat. If the bowler has conceded a no-ball or a wide, his team incurs an additional penalty because that ball (i.e., delivery) has to be bowled again and hence the batting side has the opportunity to score more runs from this extra ball.

• Specialist roles

Captain (cricket) and Wicket-keeper

The captain is often the most experienced player in the team, certainly the most tactically astute, and can possess any of the main skillsets as a batter, a bowler or a wicket-keeper. Within the Laws, the captain has certain responsibilities in terms of nominating his players to the umpires before the match and ensuring that his players conduct themselves "within the spirit and traditions of the game as well as within the Laws".

The wicket-keeper (sometimes called simply the "keeper") is a specialist fielder subject to various rules within the Laws about his equipment and demeanour. He is the only member of the fielding side who can effect a stumping and is the only one permitted to wear gloves and external leg guards. Depending on their primary skills, the other ten players in the team tend to be classified as specialist batters or specialist bowlers. Generally, a team will include five or six specialist batters and four or five specialist bowlers, plus the wicket-keeper.

- Umpires and scorers

Umpire (cricket), Scoring (cricket), and Cricket statistics

An umpire signals a decision to the scorers

The game on the field is regulated by the two umpires, one of whom stands behind the wicket at the bowler's end, the other in a position called "square leg" which is about 15–20 metres away from the batter on strike and in line with the popping crease on which he is taking guard. The umpires have several responsibilities including adjudication on whether a ball has been correctly bowled (i.e., not a no-ball or a wide); when a run is scored; whether a batter is out (the fielding side must first appeal to the umpire, usually with the phrase "How's that?" or "Owzat?"); when intervals start and end; and the suitability of the pitch, field and weather for playing the game. The umpires are authorised to interrupt or even abandon a match due to circumstances likely to endanger the players, such as a damp pitch or deterioration of the light.

Off the field in televised matches, there is usually a third umpire who can make decisions on certain incidents with the aid of video evidence. The third umpire is mandatory under the playing conditions for Test and Limited Overs International matches played between two ICC full member countries. These matches also have a match referee whose job is to ensure that play is within the Laws and the spirit of the game.

The match details, including runs and dismissals, are recorded by two official scorers, one representing each team. The scorers are directed by the hand signals of an umpire . For example, the umpire raises a forefinger to signal that the batter is out (has been dismissed); he raises both arms above his head if the batter has hit the ball for six runs. The scorers are required by the Laws to record all runs scored, wickets taken and overs bowled; in practice, they also note significant amounts of additional data relating to the game.

A match's statistics are summarised on a scorecard. Prior to the popularisation of scorecards, most scoring was done by men sitting on vantage points cuttings notches on tally sticks and runs were originally called notches.According to Rowland Bowen, the earliest known scorecard templates were introduced in 1776 by T. Pratt of Sevenoaks and soon came into general use.It is believed that scorecards were printed and sold at Lord's for the first time in 1846.

- thank you for buy & read this book

  have a great day of your
  from : Mr Vivek Kumar Pandey